英語総合教材

AROUND THE GLOBE
New Trends and Old Traditions

異文化理解のための総合英語

Masamichi Asama
Iwao Yamashita
Derek Eberl

NAN'UN-DO

AROUND THE GLOBE
New Trends and Old Traditions

Copyright © 2010

by

Masamichi Asama
Iwao Yamashita
Derek Eberl

All Rights Reserved

No part of this book may be reproduced in any form without written permission from the authors and Nan'un-do Co., Ltd.

まえがき

　英語学習のテキストで扱われる異文化学習の素材とは、とかく英米圏に比重が置かれがちです。本書はそういった傾向を打破し、学習者が広く世界中の文化に目を向けることを可能にするために編んだ大学用英語総合教材です。扱う国も、昨今の大学の標準授業時間数の履行を視野に入れ、ヴァリエーション溢れる15ヵ国を取り上げるなど、その質・分量双方においての実質化を意図しました。かといって、扱う国の数が多くなればなるほど、往々にして当該国の表面的特徴を扱うだけの教材になりかねないという危惧もあり、魅力ある学習素材の配列・配置に腐心した次第です。

　それぞれのUnitの流れに関しては、Cultural Recognition（異文化への認知）→ Cultural Awareness（異文化特性の覚醒）→ Cultural Interaction（相互文化理解）→ Follow-up Exercises（補強演習）といった4つのステージを用意し、各々のUnitで扱われるTopicへの一貫学習が自然に行われるよう配慮しました。またCultural Interactionでは、その発話部は実態に応じて米国式綴り字法もしくは英国式綴り字法を適宜採用しています。加えて、各ステージでは、文整序、正誤問題、主題選定、語彙学習、和文英訳、対話演習、聴解演習など多岐に亘る設問を用意し、英語リテラシーが総合的に深まってゆくよう工夫を凝らしました。

　本テキストで扱った15ヵ国の国々の未だ知られざる文化的・社会的側面に、多様な演習を通じて自然と親しみ、異文化理解および国際理解への新たな意識啓発へとつながれば、甚だ幸いなところです。

　最後に、この教材の作成に際しては、南雲堂の加藤敦氏・青木泰祐氏に多大なご尽力をいただきました。ここにあらためて感謝申し上げる次第です。

2010年1月

編著者　　淺間正通　山下巖　Derek Eberl

CONTENTS

Unit 1	**AUSTRALIA: Flexible School Traditions** オーストラリア：「寛容」という名の教育	6
Unit 2	**CHINA: Youth Culture** 中国：若者文化の台頭	10
Unit 3	**FINLAND: Perspectives in Learning** フィンランド：学びの本質	14
Unit 4	**GERMANY: Eco-Consciousness** ドイツ：エコ意識への目覚め	18
Unit 5	**ICELAND: Global Warming Threat** アイスランド：忍び寄る温暖化	22
Unit 6	**INDONESIA: A Comfortable Moment** インドネシア：癒しの時間	26
Unit 7	**ITALY: Historical Sites** イタリア：名所旧跡の意外性	30
Unit 8	**KOREA: Leisure Time** 韓国：余暇の今昔	34
Unit 9	**KUWAIT: Western Influence** クウェート：西洋化への憧憬	38
Unit 10	**RUSSIA: A New Cultural Stream** ロシア：新たな文化の潮流	42
Unit 11	**SPAIN: A New Trend in Culture** スペイン：伝統文化の柔軟性	46
Unit 12	**TANZANIA: Cultural Conflict** タンザニア：異文化との衝突	50
Unit 13	**THAILAND: The National Symbol** タイ：伝統へのこだわり	54
Unit 14	**THE UNITED KINGDOM: Ghosts, Fireworks, and Pubs** イギリス：娯楽を愛する精神性	58
Unit 15	**THE UNITED STATES: Security Measures** アメリカ：防犯意識の高揚	62

Unit 1

AUSTRALIA:
Flexible School Traditions

【Cultural Recognition】

 写真を参考にして、次の出だしの英文に続く内容となるよう正しくパラグラフを構成しなさい。

　　Secondary schools in Australia have many events that we Japanese could never imagine.

A. For example, there is a day called Muck-up Day when graduating students are allowed to mess up their school. It is believed that by doing this students can avoid a future life of crime.

B. This event is held just once a year on the last day before graduation, and students eagerly await their chance to take part.

C. Muck-up Day is very popular, with common tricks or pranks on this day including hanging toilet paper all over the school, throwing eggs at buildings, painting graffiti, and spraying things with water pistols.

1. (　) → 2. (　) → 3. (　)

前の問題で理解した内容にもとづいて、次の各英文の内容が正しければTを、誤っていればFを選びなさい。

1. T F Muck-up Day is an event most Japanese can relate to.
2. T F It is believed that students who take part in Muck-up Day will not commit crimes in the future.
3. T F Some students actually write on the school buildings.
4. T F Muck-up Day is a biannual event.
5. T F Many students look forward to Muck-up Day.

1.(　) 2.(　) 3.(　) 4.(　) 5.(　)

【Cultural Awareness】　次の英文を読んで下記の各設問に答えなさい。　

　Have you ever heard of a "bad hair day"? That's a day when your hair seems unmanageable and you have a bad day as a result. But at primary schools in Australia, Bad Hair Day is a day when students are allowed to come to school with their hair looking wild and unique. Parents eagerly try to make their children a standout. Of course, wearing their hair like that is banned in the school rules. But there is a good reason behind Bad Hair Day. Students must pay a few dollars for breaking the rules, and that money goes toward helping children with serious diseases. This type of fun fundraising event might be a good idea for Japanese schools, too.　(120 words)

 上記の文の内容を最も適切に表していると思われる主題を選びなさい。

1. Australian Popular Culture
2. Students Go Wild
3. Breaking the Rules
4. Bad Hair for a Good Cause　　　　　　　　　　　　　　(　)

4 下線部のアルファベットは、それぞれの英文定義にもとづく語を自由に並べ換えたものです。正しい語を空欄に綴りなさい。

1. rypimar (adj) → (　　　　　　　　)
   relating to the education of children between five and eleven years old

2. stndaotu (n) → (　　　　　　　　)
   something very noticeable because it is better or more impressive

3. rgfuaindins (n) → (　　　　　　　　)
   the activity of collecting money for a specific purpose, especially in order to help people in need

【Cultural Interaction】 次の対話文を読んでから下記の各設問に答えなさい。

背景情報 ‖ 夏期教職員研修視察でオーストラリアを訪れている高校教師の由美は、研修先で知り合った教師 Kelly から見せられた、学校行事に関する１枚のアルバム写真に目が止まりました。

Yumi: This picture is really interesting. Why are all the students in pyjamas?

Kelly: Oh, that was my class last year on Pyjama Day. All of my students dressed up, and we won a prize.

Yumi: Is that right? What kind of prize did you win?

Kelly: We won the prize for the most participation. It was a lot of fun. Practically the whole school got involved, and 1.(the / wore / his / even / principal / pyjamas) and night cap.

Yumi: That sounds great. 2.(we / like / something / had / that / wish / I) in Japan.

Kelly: It's really an exciting event, and it's for a great cause. We raised a lot of money for helping children with serious illnesses.

5 上の会話文中の 1, 2 の (　　) 内の語を意味が通るように正しく並べ換えなさい。

1. _____

2. _____

6 次の和文を英訳しなさい。

私の学校では多くの生徒が「パジャマの日」に参加しました。

_____

【Follow-up Exercises】

7 CDの英文を聴いたのち、その最も適切な応答表現の記号を答えなさい。　4

1. a. Yes, it's near Sydney Harbour Bridge.
   b. Probably about 10 minutes on foot.
   c. I think it's the Sydney Opera House.　　　　　　　　　　　(　)

2. a. It's an Aboriginal didgeridoo.
   b. No, I can't play the guitar.
   c. Yes, people in Australia like music very much.　　　　　　(　)

3. a. Vegemite's okay, but it just takes a little time to get used to it.
   b. Yes, cricket is the national sport of Australia.
   c. She sure does. She had three pieces already.　　　　　　(　)

4. a. Yes, *Crocodile Dundee* is one of my favourite movies.
   b. To be honest, there aren't many of them around here.
   c. Yes, baby kangaroos are called joeys.　　　　　　　　　　(　)

5. a. His name is Mark and he's from Brisbane.
   b. At the zoo. You can hold koalas there.
   c. It was named after Queen Victoria.　　　　　　　　　　　(　)

___

<u>Notes for Reading</u>

　　mess up「～（内）を取り散らかす」　**prank(s)**「たちの悪いいたずら」　**ban** = prohibit

<u>Notes for Listening</u>

　　didgeridoo [dìdʒəridúː]「オーストラリア先住民が使用するユーカリの木の内部をくり抜いた木筒吹奏楽器」
　　vegemite「ベジマイト（野菜エキスでつくったペースト）」　**to be honest**「率直に言って、実は」　**Queen Victoria**「ビクトリア女王（英国女王：1837-1901）」

Unit 2

CHINA:
Youth Culture

【Cultural Recognition】

 写真を参考にして、次の出だしの英文に続く内容となるよう正しくパラグラフを構成しなさい。

　　Faithful to an old Chinese tradition, many young couples all over China climb certain mountains and buy a "lovers' lock" as a way to "lock up" their love for each other. First, they have their names, the date, and their vows to each other engraved on the lock.

A. Then, so that no one can ever open the lock and thus break their eternal love, the lovers throw away the key.

B. Next, they hang their lock on an iron chain attached to a handrail, where it becomes part of a link and a symbol of their everlasting love.

C. This practice is something of a nuisance, however, as the growing number of locks at many historical places and scenic areas throughout China are rapidly becoming an eyesore.

1. (　　) → 2. (　　) → 3. (　　)

前の問題で理解した内容にもとづいて、次の各英文の内容が正しければＴを、誤っていればＦを選びなさい。

1. T F　In China, many young couples buy locks as an expression of their eternal love for each other.
2. T F　They then have their names, birthdates, and addresses printed on their locks.
3. T F　The locks prevent people from entering historical places and scenic areas.
4. T F　Couples throw away the key to their lock so that nobody can break their love.
5. T F　The locks are now regarded as a welcome addition to the natural beauty of many areas.

　　　　　　　　　　　　1. (　) 2. (　) 3. (　) 4. (　) 5. (　)

【Cultural Awareness】　　次の英文を読んで下記の各設問に答えなさい。　 5

　Today, discount coupons can be found in most magazines. But young Chinese people now have a new way to get discounts. In the major underground stations of Shanghai, you will often see a machine called a VELO, which looks like an ATM (Automatic Teller Machine). In order to use the machine, you have to get a VELO CARD beforehand. These cards are issued free of charge. If you touch the sensor panel with your card and click the buttons of the shops, restaurants, bookstores, cinemas, and so on that you are interested in, the machine will print out the desired discount coupons. As saving money is always a major concern for young people everywhere, it is likely that similar machines will soon gain popularity in other countries, too.　　　　　　　　　　　　　　　　　(128 words)

 上記の文の内容を最も適切に表していると思われる主題を選びなさい。

1. A New ATM
2. Shanghai's New Subway System
3. A Discount Dispenser
4. How to Save Money　　　　　　　　　　　　　　　　　　　(　)

4 下線部のアルファベットは、それぞれの英文定義にもとづく語を自由に並べ換えたものです。正しい語を空欄に綴りなさい。

1. sdincotu (n) → (　　　　　　　　　)
   a reduction in the usual price of something

2. cghare (n) → (　　　　　　　　　)
   the amount of money paid for goods or services

3. ocnernc (n) → (　　　　　　　　　)
   something that is important to you or that involves you

【Cultural Interaction】 次の対話文を読んでから下記の各設問に答えなさい。

背景情報｜日本の大手機械メーカーに勤める鈴木氏は、商用で中国の現地工場を訪れました。現地工場責任者の Mr. Chen の流暢な英語による施設案内に感嘆しきりです。

Suzuki: Mr. Chen, I really envy you because you speak such wonderful English. 1.(did / become / fluent / so / how / you)?

Chen: Actually, when I was a college student, I studied in the United States for several years.

Suzuki: Do a lot of Chinese students study abroad?

Chen: Yes, and the trend is growing. Many companies are looking for new employees who can speak a foreign language and 2.(experience / have / who / abroad / living).

Suzuki: Do many Chinese students come to Japanese universities, too?

Chen: Yes. In fact, my nephew is now studying at a university in Kyoto. He's majoring in business management. He really likes it there.

5 上の会話文中の 1, 2 の (　　) 内の語を意味が通るように正しく並べ換えなさい。

1. _____

2. _____

6 次の和文を英訳しなさい。

私の姪は中国の大学で東洋史を専攻しています。

_____

【Follow-up Exercises】

7 CDの英文を聴いたのち、その最も適切な応答表現の記号を答えなさい。　　7

1. a. It's really not that big.
   b. I'm not sure, but it took many years to build.
   c. We were in Beijing for three days.　　(　)

2. a. I used to practice Chinese calligraphy in school.
   b. I see some students training in the park early in the morning.
   c. Tai chi is practiced by many people throughout the country.　　(　)

3. a. I have no idea, but I think Chinese food is really delicious.
   b. He bought some traditional tea cups and pots at a gift shop in Shanghai.
   c. We bought this fish at the market this morning.　　(　)

4. a. Not really, because he is a very strange person.
   b. Some of them, because they are used in Japan, too.
   c. He's my favorite character in that comic book.　　(　)

5. a. It looks like him. He was my best friend in grade school.
   b. I can't remember what time we came back.
   c. No, but I want to learn it while I'm studying in China.　　(　)

Notes for Reading

　　engrave「(文字などを)刻む、彫る」　scenic areas「風光明媚な観光地」　eyesore「目ざわり」

Notes for Listening

　　Beijing [bèidʒíŋ]「北京」　calligraphy「書道」　tai chi [tái dʒíː]「太極拳」　Shanghai「上海」

Unit 3

FINLAND:
Perspectives in Learning

【Cultural Recognition】

 写真を参考にして、次の出だしの英文に続く内容となるよう正しくパラグラフを構成しなさい。

  Finland is a country with thousands of lakes and islands. Ferries are such an important means of transportation there that people usually consider them an extension of the roads.

A. Although there are several kinds of ferries, one type, called a "lossi" in Finnish, is particularly popular amongst people who live in remote areas.

B. This is because the lossi not only run on schedule, but also because they connect inhabitants of offshore islands to the mainland free of charge, taking their vehicles and bicycles with them.

C. Although Finland is noted for its advanced technology, the country's ferries are a romantic reminder of the past.

        1. (　) → 2. (　) → 3. (　)

前の問題で理解した内容にもとづいて、次の各英文の内容が正しければTを、誤っていればFを選びなさい。

1. T F　Finland's landscape is a glorious combination of lakes and islands.
2. T F　Ferries are important in Finland because there are so few roads.
3. T F　The lossi are an important means of transportation for Finnish people who live in isolated places.
4. T F　The cost of riding a lossi depends on how far you travel.
5. T F　Finland's ferries symbolize the country's advanced technology.

　　　　　　　　　　1. (　) 2. (　) 3. (　) 4. (　) 5. (　)

【Cultural Awareness】　次の英文を読んで下記の各設問に答えなさい。 8

　Ever since students in Finland emerged as top performers in the Organization for Economic Cooperation and Development's Programme for International Student Assessment (PISA), many people in Japan have begun to take note of this Scandinavian country and of how the Finns educate their children. What's so special about schools in Finland? The experts are unanimous in saying that in Finland teachers help children learn on their own, rather than just give them facts and figures. This means that the aim of education there is essentially to nurture character and instill a sense of independence, whereas in Japan, many students study to achieve high scores on high-school and university entrance exams. It may be that the time has come for Japanese teachers and policymakers to take a good, hard look at Japan's education system.　　　　　　　　　　　(133 words)

 上記の文の内容を最も適切に表していると思われる主題を選びなさい。

1. A Finnish Model for Japan's Education System
2. Educational Trends around the Globe
3. Educating Hearts and Minds
4. How to Perform Well on the PISA　　　　　　　　　　　　(　)

4 下線部のアルファベットは、それぞれの英文定義にもとづく語を自由に並べ換えたものです。正しい語を空欄に綴りなさい。

1. nmiauosun (adj) → (   )
   fully in agreement

2. oeiudactn (n) → (   )
   the process of teaching, training, and learning

3. ndeeeepndinc (n) → (   )
   making your own decisions without relying on other people

【Cultural Interaction】 次の対話文を読んでから下記の各設問に答えなさい。

背景情報 | 交換留学生としてフィンランドの大学に通う日本人留学生の真理は、クラスメートのJohannaが持っている携帯電話に関心を抱いています。次第に話題は、授業態度の違いへと進展していきます。

Mari: I really like the design of your mobile phone. What kind is it?

Johanna: It's a Nokia. It's quite handy and has a wide variety of functions.

Mari: Do a lot of Finnish students have mobile phones like we do in Japan?

Johanna: Yes, practically everyone has one. The only difference here is that 1.(at / school / them / use / to / rarely / are / able / students), especially during class time.

Mari: I know what you mean. Students here really have to participate in class and give their opinions on different subjects. It's a lot different from Japan.

Johanna: Well, you've had no trouble adjusting to your classes here. 2.(quite / well / to / you / doing / seem / be).

5 上の会話文中の 1, 2 の (   ) 内の語を意味が通るように正しく並べ換えなさい。

1. _____

2. _____

6 次の和文を英訳しなさい。

フィンランドの大学生は公共交通機関の中ではマナーモードで携帯電話を使用しますか？

_____

【Follow-up Exercises】

7 CDの英文を聴いたのち、その最も適切な応答表現の記号を答えなさい。　🔊 10

1. a. Yes, I know her. Her name is Helmi.
   b. Yes, he has a very nice computer at home.
   c. Everyone here learns quite a bit about them at school.　　　　（　）

2. a. I think he left at about six o'clock this morning.
   b. He likes to go to the library after work.
   c. I'm not sure. I think he's from Helsinki.　　　　（　）

3. a. We stayed up very late last night.
   b. They are going to the sauna later this afternoon.
   c. I don't know. I hope nothing happened.　　　　（　）

4. a. Yes, I think it's time to go.
   b. It's a beautiful, large, hand-made clock.
   c. I'm sorry. I don't have a watch on.　　　　（　）

5. a. I heard it from a friend who works there.
   b. They will be arriving the day after tomorrow.
   c. Male students study science.　　　　（　）

_____

<u>**Notes for Reading**</u>

remote area(s)「人里離れた場所、へんぴな場所」　**emerge**「明らかになる」　**PISA**「(OECD 主催による) 国際学習到達度調査」　**take note of**「～に注目する」　**nurture**「～を育む」　**instill**「～(の精神など) を植え付ける」

<u>**Notes for Listening**</u>

Helsinki「ヘルシンキ (フィンランドの首都；人口約 56 万人)」　**stay up late**「夜遅くまでおきている」　**have ～ on**「～を身につけている」

Unit 4

GERMANY:
Eco-Consciousness

【Cultural Recognition】

  写真を参考にして、次の出だしの英文に続く内容となるよう正しくパラグラフを構成しなさい。

   The Berlin Tramway is one of the oldest and largest tram networks in the world. It began in 1865 as a horse bus running between two terminals.

A. This short route quickly evolved into an extensive tram network that branched out throughout the city.

B. Today, however, in many parts of Europe, trams are making a comeback and are once again becoming the preferred means of transportation.

C. For nearly a century, people commuted on the trams, but with the rise of the automobile in the mid-20th century, their popularity began to decrease not only in Berlin but worldwide.

1. (　) → 2. (　) → 3. (　)

前の問題で理解した内容にもとづいて、次の各英文の内容が正しければTを、誤っていればFを選びなさい。

1. T F　Berlin's tram system initially had only one route.
2. T F　Berlin's tram network declined in popularity because it didn't run throughout the city.
3. T F　Trams are again becoming popular in Europe.
4. T F　Berlin's tram system is still the same as it was when it began in 1865.
5. T F　Trams were a means of transportation long before the automobile.

1.(　) 2.(　) 3.(　) 4.(　) 5.(　)

【Cultural Awareness】　次の英文を読んで下記の各設問に答えなさい。

　Germany has been experiencing a remarkable boom in the use of solar energy since the beginning of the 21st century. In 2006, the German government introduced a "feed-in" tariff system. Under this system, power companies are required to buy electricity generated by energy suppliers at a fixed price. The system has also worked as an effective measure for the promotion of solar-power generation and use. According to the Solar Energy Association, in 2005, in terms of solar-panel production, Germany had already overtaken Japan, which had been the world's front-runner in the field of solar-energy development. It is not too much to say that the time has come for Japan to switch over to the kind of alternative energy and environmental policies adopted by Germany.

(126 words)

 上記の文の内容を最も適切に表していると思われる主題を選びなさい。

1. Energy at a Fixed Price
2. German Success in Solar-power Use
3. Japan No Longer Number One
4. German Solar-panel Production　　　　　　　　　　(　)

4 下線部のアルファベットは、それぞれの英文定義にもとづく語を自由に並べ換えたものです。正しい語を空欄に綴りなさい。

1. egtnreae (v) → (   )
   to produce energy or electric power

2. ciper (n) → (   )
   the amount of money paid for something

3. tcsiwh (v) → (   )
   to change the position of something

【Cultural Interaction】 次の対話文を読んでから下記の各設問に答えなさい。

背景情報 ドイツの自動車メーカーにインターンシップ留学している友彦は、週末に職場の同僚 Fritz に誘われてドライブに行きました。高級車は燃費が悪いというイメージを抱いていた友彦の話題から日独自動車談義へと話が進展していきます。

Tomo: Your BMW doesn't seem to use much gas. Does it have a hybrid engine?

Fritz: Yes, it does. ₁.(fuel / diesel / runs / on / it / both / and / electricity). What about your car? I hear that in Japan there are many hybrid vehicles on the road these days.

Tomo: Actually, the car I have now runs on regular gasoline, but I would like to buy a hybrid vehicle sometime in the near future.

Fritz: Are you planning on buying a Toyota Prius? I hear they are one of the top-selling hybrid vehicles in the world.

Tomo: Yes, I would like to get one. They have a good reputation and, compared to other cars, are very environmentally friendly.

Fritz: That's good. I think protecting the environment is important.
₂.(many / drive / so / people / since / cars), everyone should start thinking about driving a hybrid vehicle.

5 上の会話文中の 1, 2 の（ ）内の語を意味が通るように正しく並べ換えなさい。

1. _____

2. _____

6 次の和文を英訳しなさい。

日本製の車はドイツ製の車と比べると低燃費です。

_____

【Follow-up Exercises】

7 CDの英文を聴いたのち、その最も適切な応答表現の記号を答えなさい。　🎧 13

1. a. It is, but I still think it's too expensive.
   b. He used to drive a Mercedes Benz.
   c. Thank you. I brush them every day.　　　　　　　　　（　　）

2. a. He said he's going to go there later.
   b. She must have heard us talking about it this morning.
   c. It's going to be at a beer garden along the Rhine.　　　（　　）

3. a. I think in late September.
   b. It was a great time. German beer is the best.
   c. He began last year, but hasn't finished yet.　　　　　　（　　）

4. a. I didn't eat them. I don't know who did.
   b. He cooked the wieners on a barbecue grill.
   c. I've already had some, thank you. They were excellent.　（　　）

5. a. Yes, she lives in Hamburg.
   b. Sure. Let me write it down for you.
   c. No, I can't go because I have to work.　　　　　　　　（　　）

Notes for Reading

an extensive tram network「広域路面電車交通網」　**branch out throughout the city**「市内を縦横無尽に駆け巡る」　**commute**「通勤する」　**a "feed-in" tariff system**「固定価格買取制度」　**effective measure**「有効な手段」　**alternative energy**「代替エネルギー」　**BMW**「ビー・エム・ダブリュー（ドイツの高級車；Bayerische Motoren Werke = Bavarian Motor Works）」

Notes for Listening

Mercedes Benz [mərséidiːz bénz]「メルセデスベンツ（ドイツの高級車）」**the Rhine**「ライン川（スイスアルプスに端を発し、ドイツを南から北へと流れる大河）」　**weiner(s)** [wéiːnər]「ウィンナーソーセージ」

Unit 5

ICELAND:
Global Warming Threat

【Cultural Recognition】

 写真を参考にして、次の出だしの英文に続く内容となるよう正しくパラグラフを構成しなさい。

 A glacier is a large, slow-moving river of ice, formed from compacted layers of snow.

A. The most famous glacier in Iceland is Vatnajokull, which covers an area of 8,000 square kilometers and is, at its deepest point, more than 900 meters thick.

B. But some experts say that the glacier is now melting at a rate of a meter a year, and that climate change could quicken its loss.

C. This melting implies that in the future, people all over the world might have to migrate to higher places because of rising sea levels and coastal flooding.

1. (　) → 2. (　) → 3. (　)

前の問題で理解した内容にもとづいて、次の各英文の内容が正しければTを、誤っていればFを選びなさい。

1. T F   Glaciers are formed when rainwater turns into ice.
2. T F   Vatnajokull is a lake which is always frozen over.
3. T F   Some people think that global warming is a serious threat to the Vatnajokull Glacier.
4. T F   Global warming is closely related to rising sea levels.
5. T F   People may have to move away from coastal areas if climate change continues.

1. (　) 2. (　) 3. (　) 4. (　) 5. (　)

【Cultural Awareness】　　次の英文を読んで下記の各設問に答えなさい。

Whale watching is becoming an increasingly popular tourist attraction in Iceland. The reason behind this phenomenon is that global warming is now beginning to affect the econiche of the Icelandic coast. As the waters around the country warm, whales no longer need to migrate south in order to find food and give birth. They can now spend the entire year near Iceland. This may be good for whale-watching companies, but the impact that global warming will have on a wider scale remains to be seen, though it is highly likely that other animal species are also being affected by this change.

(101 words)

 上記の文の内容を最も適切に表していると思われる主題を選びなさい。

1. Whale-watching Tours of Iceland
2. Iceland's Coastal Waters
3. Whale Migration Patterns
4. Whale Watching and Global Warming　　　　　　　　　(　)

23

4

下線部のアルファベットは、それぞれの英文定義にもとづく語を自由に並べ換えたものです。正しい語を空欄に綴りなさい。

1. triouts (n) → (   )
   a person who is traveling or visiting a place for pleasure

2. blalgo (adj) → (   )
   covering or affecting the whole world

3. lcsea (n) → (   )
   the size or extent of something

【Cultural Interaction】

次の対話文を読んでから下記の各設問に答えなさい。

背景情報：国際環境ボランティアのメンバーとして活動する日本人大学生の健一は、同じく活動メンバーとして顔見知りのアイスランド人大学生 Thor と国際電話で意見交換しています。

Kenichi: I read somewhere that polar bears are able to swim quite far and sometimes swim the 300 kilometers from Greenland to Iceland. Is that true?

Thor: Well, in a way that's right. There have been reports of polar bears swimming all the way here, but some scientists believe that 1.(the / swim / way / whole / the / bears / don't / actually).

Kenichi: What do you mean? Then how do they get here? Do they take a boat?

Thor: Very funny! No, it seems more likely that many of them travel on icebergs most of the way and then swim to shore.

Kenichi: That's really interesting.

Thor: Yes, it is. But it also has a lot of people worried. 2.(seems / in / ice / there / be / to / increase /an / melting) due to global warming and, as a result, more and more polar bears are beginning to drift out to sea. There is no avoiding the fact that the natural environment is changing.

5

上の会話文中の 1, 2 の（   ）内の語を意味が通るように正しく並べ換えなさい。

1. _____

2. _____

6 次の和文を英訳しなさい。

最近の動物園では、北極熊の飼育が次第に困難になってきています。

_____

【Follow-up Exercises】

7 CDの英文を聴いたのち、その最も適切な応答表現の記号を答えなさい。　16

1. a. I'll tell you after we're finished.
   b. I recommend the fish. It's quite delicious.
   c. When they arrive later tonight.　　　　　　　　　　　(　)

2. a. It can't be helped. Iceland is a cold place.
   b. It wasn't me. He turned off the heater.
   c. I've only been waiting a few minutes.　　　　　　　 (　)

3. a. They are doing fine. Thank you.
   b. They like to play a lot of chess.
   c. I'm busy tomorrow, but how about Tuesday?　　　　(　)

4. a. No, the capital is Reykjavik.
   b. Let me check the map again.
   c. The answer is wrong. It's left, not right.　　　　　 (　)

5. a. Actually, they don't celebrate Christmas.
   b. We took a nice long holiday together.
   c. On March 1st, Beer Day.　　　　　　　　　　　　 (　)

Notes for Reading

formed from compacted layers of snow「いくつもの雪の断層から成る」　**phenomenon**「現象、事象」（複数形は **phenomena**）　**econiche**「生態的地位」　**migrate**「移動する」　**entire year**「一年中」　**animal species**「（種としての）動物」　**drift out**「漂流する」

Notes for Listening

Reykjavik「レイキャビク（アイスランドの首都；人口約16万人）」　**Beer Day**「ビールの日（アイスランドでは、1989年3月1日にビールが解禁された）」

Unit 6

INDONESIA:
A Comfortable Moment

【Cultural Recognition】

写真を参考にして、次の出だしの英文に続く内容となるよう正しくパラグラフを構成しなさい。

As you can see, these three Indonesian boys are enjoying bathing in a pond near their home.

A. Mandi helps both children and adults keep cool and refreshed and can be enjoyed at home as well as in the open air.

B. You will seldom meet an Indonesian who doesn't take advantage of the state of genuine bliss that a Mandi bath offers.

C. This is not your ordinary dip in a pool, however, but is a unique kind of bathing called Mandi, a time-honored tradition among the people of Indonesia.

1. (　) → 2. (　) → 3. (　)

前の問題で理解した内容にもとづいて、次の各英文の内容が正しければTを、誤っていればFを選びなさい。

1. T F　Bathing similar to the Mandi can be found everywhere.
2. T F　A Mandi bath keeps people comfortable and happy.
3. T F　It is rare to meet an Indonesian who doesn't enjoy a Mandi bath.
4. T F　Mandi is a fairly recent custom.
5. T F　Most Indonesians stop taking a Mandi bath when they grow up.

　　　　　　　　　　1. (　) 2. (　) 3. (　) 4. (　) 5. (　)

【Cultural Awareness】　次の英文を読んで下記の各設問に答えなさい。

Open-air barbershops are still popular in small towns in Indonesia. The barber usually just stops his motorbike along the roadside and quickly sets up shop under a shade tree. His "shop" is nothing but a simple stool on which his customers sit. That's it. The atmosphere of the Indonesian open-air barbershop is casual and friendly. The price of a shave and haircut isn't set, but is decided by negotiation between the barber and the customer, which they both enjoy very much. Of course, there are ordinary barbershops in Indonesia as well. But some Indonesian people prefer the open-air type. They love the atmosphere and get a real kick out of chatting with the barber.

(114 words)

 上記の文の内容を最も適切に表していると思われる主題を選びなさい。

1. By the Roadside
2. More than Just a Haircut
3. Ordinary Barbershops
4. How to Negotiate with Your Barber　　　　　　　　(　)

27

下線部のアルファベットは、それぞれの英文定義にもとづく語を自由に並べ換えたものです。正しい語を空欄に綴りなさい。

1. scaalu (adj) → (　　　　　　　　　)
   relaxed and not worried; informal

2. taigotnineo (n) → (　　　　　　　　　)
   discussion or compromise

3. ucstoerm (n) → (　　　　　　　　　)
   someone who buys goods or services from a shop, company, etc.

【Cultural Interaction】　次の対話文を読んでから下記の各設問に答えなさい。

背景情報 ‖ インドネシア人のEddiと国際結婚した佳奈子は未だ現地の生活に馴染めないでいます。そんな佳奈子に夫のEddiは日本の文化との違いを説明しています。

Eddi:　　What are you doing back so soon? I thought you were going to get something to eat. What happened?

Kanako:　I was, but my favorite food stall is closed today. I don't understand. I went there last week on the same day and at the same time and it was open.

Eddi:　　Well, you know 1.(don't / many / keep / places / a / time / fixed) for doing business here. They close whenever they want, and open whenever they want.

Kanako:　Really? Why is that? It's very frustrating.

Eddi:　　I suppose it is, but here the concept of time is quite different than in many other places. In Indonesian culture, 2.(believe / flexible / is / that / people / time). That's why you often hear the expression "jam karet," which means "rubber time."

Kanako:　That's an interesting concept, but I think it's going to take me some time to get used to living here in Indonesia.

 上の会話文中の1,2の(　　)内の語を意味が通るように正しく並べ換えなさい。

1. _____

2. _____

6 次の和文を英訳しなさい。

日本とインドネシアでは時間の概念がずいぶん異なると耳にしますが本当ですか。

_____

【Follow-up Exercises】

7 CDの英文を聴いたのち、その最も適切な応答表現の記号を答えなさい。　🎧 19

1. a. I think Martha would be interested.
   b. I've seen that movie more than once.
   c. No, thank you. I'm already full.　　　　　　　　　　( )

2. a. They should be in Jakarta soon.
   b. I didn't know there were so many islands.
   c. A package from home with some presents.　　　　　( )

3. a. She used to live there a few years ago.
   b. I told you. I've been there three times.
   c. Don't worry. I'm sure many people will be late.　　( )

4. a. Let's go by car.
   b. I picked up some spices there this morning.
   c. There are quite a few in this area.　　　　　　　　　( )

5. a. Yes, he had fruit for breakfast this morning.
   b. I don't think so. What is it?
   c. She only knows how to cook one dish.　　　　　　　( )

<u>Notes for Reading</u>
　　set up「設置する」　**under a shade tree**「木陰で」　**nothing but**「〜にしか過ぎない」　**stool**「(肘掛、背もたれのない1人用の) 腰かけ」　**atmosphere**「雰囲気」　**get a kick out of**「〜を心から楽しむ」　**food stall**「屋台」

<u>Notes for Listening</u>
　　Jakarta「ジャカルタ」

29

Unit 7

ITALY:
Historical Sites

【Cultural Recognition】

 写真を参考にして、次の出だしの英文に続く内容となるよう正しくパラグラフを構成しなさい。

　　The Colosseum, one of the most impressive monuments of the Roman Empire, is visited annually by millions of international tourists, who like to go inside to look at the arena.

A. The games usually ended with a fight to the death between an animal and a gladiator, or between two gladiators.

B. But today, the site has become a symbol of the sanctity of life and highlights Italy's support for a global ban on the death penalty. The Colosseum's arches light up when Italy celebrates another country's decision to abolish capital punishment.

C. In ancient Rome, emperors used the Colosseum to entertain the public with free sports and games, which usually began with an exotic animal show.

1. (　　) → 2. (　　) → 3. (　　)

前の問題で理解した内容にもとづいて、次の各英文の内容が正しければTを、誤っていればFを選びなさい。

1. T F　The Colosseum is a popular tourist attraction for people all over the world.
2. T F　Tourists can still enjoy animal shows and clashes between gladiators at the Colosseum.
3. T F　In ancient Rome, not only animals but also many people lost their lives in the Colosseum.
4. T F　The Colosseum has become a symbol of Italy's opposition to capital punishment.
5. T F　The death penalty has now been banned around the globe.

1.(　) 2.(　) 3.(　) 4.(　) 5.(　)

【Cultural Awareness】　次の英文を読んで下記の各設問に答えなさい。 20

Trevi Fountain, one of the most beautiful fountains in the world, is famous for its many legends. According to the most popular, throwing a coin over your shoulder into the fountain ensures that you will return to Rome in the future. The fountain also has a legend concerning lovers. A girl whose lover is about to leave Rome for military service or work is assured eternal love if she makes her boyfriend drink a glass of water from the fountain and then breaks the glass. A safer way of guaranteeing eternal love is to drink from the "small fountain for lovers" next to Trevi Fountain. Lovers must drink together to ensure that they will be faithful to each other forever. Such legends add to the fountain's charm.

(127 words)

 上記の文の内容を最も適切に表していると思われる主題を選びなさい。

1. Return to Rome
2. The Beauty of Trevi Fountain
3. Legends of Trevi Fountain
4. Eternal Love

(　)

4 下線部のアルファベットは、それぞれの英文定義にもとづく語を自由に並べ換えたものです。正しい語を空欄に綴りなさい。

1. tfnouain (n) → (　　　　　　　　)
   a stream of water that is forced up into the air by a pump

2. dlngee (n) → (　　　　　　　　)
   a traditional story sometimes regarded as historically true

3. eltnera (adj) → (　　　　　　　　)
   lasting or existing forever

【Cultural Interaction】　次の対話文を読んでから下記の各設問に答えなさい。

背景情報　観光旅行でイタリアの町ピサにある世界遺産の斜塔を訪れた慶子は、現地添乗員のSabrinaからいろいろと説明を受けています。

Sabrina: Well, here it is. What do you think?

Keiko: Unbelievable. It really is a leaning tower. 1.(does / that / it / way / how / stay)? I'm surprised it hasn't fallen over.

Sabrina: Well, actually, it almost did. The tower started leaning too much, so some engineers and building experts had to fix it. They ended up straightening it up a little.

Keiko: That's interesting. 2.(must / it / lot / have / of / taken / a / work) to do that.

Sabrina: It did. The tower was closed to the public for a long time. Now it's supposed to be safe from falling for another 200 years or so.

Keiko: Well, I guess that's good news. Now I can take plenty of pictures without having to worry about it falling over on us.

5 上の会話文中の1, 2の(　　)内の語を意味が通るように正しく並べ換えなさい。

1. _____
2. _____

6 次の和文を英訳しなさい。

交通渋滞に巻き込まれ、旅行者達は飛行機に乗り遅れてしまった。

【Follow-up Exercises】

7 CDの英文を聴いたのち、その最も適切な応答表現の記号を答えなさい。 🎧 22

1. a. We left from Milan two days ago.
    b. I already know my way around the city.
    c. The last time I saw it, it was on the table.　　　　　　　　　( )

2. a. It depends on the season and the place.
    b. All the tables have a large umbrella.
    c. I've never seen so many pigeons.　　　　　　　　　　　　　( )

3. a. I don't mind as long as she can pay her own way.
    b. I've never been there, but she comes from Sicily.
    c. The wait is very long, but it's okay.　　　　　　　　　　　　( )

4. a. I'm sorry. I'm very busy tomorrow.
    b. Registered mail's the safest and fastest.
    c. It took us about three hours to get to Milan.　　　　　　　　( )

5. a. There's a flower shop down the street.
    b. That sounds like a great idea.
    c. I'm sorry. We're not taking the express.　　　　　　　　　　( )

<u>Notes for Reading</u>

　arena「闘技場」　**capital punishment**「死刑、極刑」

<u>Notes for Listening</u>

　Milan「ミラノ（イタリア北部にある工業都市）」　**pigeon**「鳩」　**Sicily**「シチリア島（イタリア南方の地中海最大の島）」　**registered mail**「書留郵便（物）」

Unit 8

KOREA:
Leisure Time

【Cultural Recognition】

1 写真を参考にして、次の出だしの英文に続く内容となるよう正しくパラグラフを構成しなさい。

　　At Korean movie theaters, you are allowed to bring in outside food and drink. So it is common to find street vendors selling foods like fried squid and waffles in front of theater box offices.

A. Going to movies at theaters used to be one of Korea's most popular holiday activities, but these days cinemas are struggling to make money.

B. There are two main reasons for this. One is that many Koreans now watch movies on PC displays at home, and the other is the result of an American request.

C. In response, the Korean government downsized the so-called screen quota, a policy which requires that a minimum of 20% of all business days be reserved exclusively for the showing of Korean films.

1. (　) → 2. (　) → 3. (　)

2

前の問題で理解した内容にもとづいて、次の各英文の内容が正しければTを、誤っていればFを選びなさい。

1. T F　It is prohibited to eat outside food and drink in movie theaters in Korea.
2. T F　It is common to see food stalls in front of theaters in Korea.
3. T F　Koreans do not watch many movies because they enjoy using computers so much more.
4. T F　Korean movie theaters are currently enjoying a period of profitability.
5. T F　Today, Korean films must be shown at least 20% of the time.

1. (　) 2. (　) 3. (　) 4. (　) 5. (　)

【Cultural Awareness】　次の英文を読んで下記の各設問に答えなさい。　23

　According to a 2007 survey released by the Ministry of Culture, Sports and Tourism of the Republic of Korea, Koreans over 18 years of age read an average of 1.8 books per month. Their Japanese counterparts read an average of 1.5 books per month. In 2006, Koreans and Japanese read an average of 1.5 and 1.4 books per month, respectively. Wait a minute! Korea has a very large Internet following, doesn't it? In fact, there's a word in Korean, "pein," which translates to "chudoku" in Japanese and "addict" in English. There are many "net-pein" (Internet addicts) in Korea. Also, writing libelous online messages about entertainment-world celebrities often results in serious social problems. Despite Korea's widespread Internet culture, it is very interesting to know that Koreans still read more paper-based material than the Japanese.

(133 words)

3

上記の文の内容を最も適切に表していると思われる主題を選びなさい。

1. Koreans Outread Japanese
2. The Importance of Reading Paper-based Books
3. The Ministry of Sports, Culture and Tourism of the Republic of Korea
4. Internet Addiction and Reading in Korea

(　)

4 下線部のアルファベットは、それぞれの英文定義にもとづく語を自由に並べ換えたものです。正しい語を空欄に綴りなさい。

1. nmitisyr (n) → (　　　　　　　　)
   a government department responsible for one area of government work, such as education or health

2. cotunerprta (n) → (　　　　　　　　)
   someone or something that has the same job or purpose as someone or something else in a different place

3. acditd (n) → (　　　　　　　　)
   someone who is overly interested in something and can't help spending a lot of time doing it

【Cultural Interaction】　次の対話文を読んでから下記の各設問に答えなさい。　24

背景情報 ‖ 日本のＩＴ系企業からの出向で韓国の支社にシステムエンジニアとして赴任している博美は、同僚の Sun が使用している真新しいノートパソコンが気になっています。

Hiromi: Hi, Sun. Did you get a new computer?

Sun: Yes. I had to because my little brother was using my old one all the time and I could never get to it. It drove me nuts.

Hiromi: What's he doing on the computer all the time? Is he studying?

Sun: No. He and his friends like playing online games. They are on the Internet all day long. To tell the truth, I think they're addicted. My mother is starting to worry about it, too.

Hiromi: Wow, that's not good. I hope 1.(grades / aren't / it / affected / being / by / their / school).

Sun: I don't know, but I never see him studying anymore. He's supposed to get his grades the day after tomorrow. 2.(mother / a shock / I / hope / my / doesn't / get).

5 上の会話文中の1, 2の(　　)内の語を意味が通るように正しく並べ換えなさい。

1. _____

2. _____

6 次の和文を英訳しなさい。

一昨日購入したゲームソフトの説明書は余りにも難解すぎてよく理解できませんでした。

___

【Follow-up Exercises】

7 CDの英文を聴いたのち、その最も適切な応答表現の記号を答えなさい。　25

1. a. I found some ginger in the drawer.
   b. The teacher lent us the key yesterday.
   c. I've only been here a few minutes.　　　　　　　　　（　）

2. a. I guess on the Internet.
   b. I hear it is near Namsan Park.
   c. The Internet cafe is quite crowded all the time.　　　（　）

3. a. No, his name is Myeoung. He's a doctor.
   b. Yes, we drank a little at the party yesterday.
   c. No, the legal drinking age is 19.　　　　　　　　　（　）

4. a. Let me check in back.
   b. Those look good on you.
   c. They're too tight.　　　　　　　　　　　　　　　（　）

5. a. Sure he did. He left the dish on the table.
   b. Really? Let me double-check with the waiter.
   c. Everyone loves eating Korean barbeque.　　　　　　（　）

___

<u>*Notes for Reading*</u>

street vendors「街頭の物売り」　**downsize**「〜の規模を縮小する」　**the so-called screen quota**「いわゆる映画上映割り当て制度」　**policy**「政策、方針」　**libelous**「誹謗中傷の」　**celebrity (pl. celebrities)**「有名人、名士」

<u>*Notes for Listening*</u>

look good on 〜「〜に似合っている」　**Korean barbecue**「韓国焼き肉」

Unit 9

KUWAIT:
Western Influence

【Cultural Recognition】

1 写真を参考にして、次の出だしの英文に続く内容となるよう正しくパラグラフを構成しなさい。

Middle Eastern countries more or less differ from each other in the degree of their tolerance for personal freedom.

A. In Kuwait, some women wear a black garment called an "abayah," while others wear a scarf-like cover called a "hejab." Children are generally free to wear any attire they like.

B. Most men, however, wear the traditional garment called a "thoub," which protects them from the blazing sun and frequent sandstorms.

C. But you can also see people wearing Western-style clothes, such as jeans for the men and dresses for the women.

1. (　) → 2. (　) → 3. (　)

2 前の問題で理解した内容にもとづいて、次の各英文の内容が正しければTを、誤っていればFを選びなさい。

1. T F　In Kuwait, only children are not allowed to wear any Western-style clothing.
2. T F　All women in Kuwait cover their faces with a "hejab."
3. T F　The traditional garment called a "thoub" evolved because of the harsh climate.
4. T F　Some Middle Eastern countries are more tolerant of personal freedom than others.
5. T F　An "abayah" is a long robe modeled on a Western dress.

1.(　) 2.(　) 3.(　) 4.(　) 5.(　)

【Cultural Awareness】　次の英文を読んで下記の各設問に答えなさい。

Kuwait's population consists of people of many different cultures. It is interesting to note that Kuwaiti citizens account for only about 40 percent of the entire population. In Kuwait, you see many foreign workers and students of different nationalities on the street. Surprisingly, most of them have a good command of English, though the official language in Kuwait is Arabic. So you can manage to live there without speaking or understanding the official language. In daily communication, for example, if you ask someone who looks local how to get to a certain destination in English, he or she will kindly answer you in the same way. It is much wiser, however, to remember the old saying, "When in Rome, do as the Romans do," and to try to learn the language.

(132 words)

3 上記の文の内容を最も適切に表していると思われる主題を選びなさい。

1. Kuwaiti Language Learning
2. Kuwait's Foreign Workers
3. No Need to Speak Arabic
4. English as Kuwait's Lingua Franca

(　)

4

下線部のアルファベットは、それぞれの英文定義にもとづく語を自由に並べ換えたものです。正しい語を空欄に綴りなさい。

1. iicntze (n) → (   )
   someone who lives in a particular town, state, or country

2. mmocnda (n) → (   )
   the ability to use knowledge, language, etc.

3. allco (adj) → (   )
   belonging to the area where you live

【Cultural Interaction】

次の対話文を読んでから下記の各設問に答えなさい。　27

背景情報 ‖ 大学の授業でクウェートの文化についてレポートを書こうと考えた俊夫は、日本への留学中に出会ったクウェート人の Jawad と次のようなメールのやり取りを通して情報を入手しています。

Toshio: The pearl diving festival in Kuwait sounds like an exciting event.

Jawad: Yes, it is. For the young men participating in it, it's a very strenuous, but rewarding experience. They really have to learn a lot about the old tradition of pearl diving and train rigorously for it.

Toshio: 1.(it / when / how / does / long / and / held / is / it) last?

Jawad: The festival usually takes place in August. But the divers have to train for weeks before the actual festival begins. There's a lot to learn.

Toshio: That's a lot of preparation. Is it a contest 2.(the / to / most / who / see / find / can / pearls)?

Jawad: Not really. Actually, the main purpose is to teach young Kuwaitis about the principal occupation of their forefathers back in the days before oil was discovered there.

5

上の会話文中の 1, 2 の（　）内の語を意味が通るように正しく並べ換えなさい。

1. _____
2. _____

6 次の和文を英訳しなさい。

私がクウェートを訪れる主な目的は、アラビア語を学ぶことです。

_____

【Follow-up Exercises】

7 CDの英文を聴いたのち、その最も適切な応答表現の記号を答えなさい。　🔊 28

1. a. That dress is beautiful.
   b. He likes fishing. He goes once a week.
   c. You can say that again.　　　　　　　　　　　　　　　　（　）

2. a. That might be it over there.
   b. Yes. Our trip is for two nights and three days.
   c. This hotel is great. It has everything.　　　　　　　　　（　）

3. a. It's a small, traditional Kuwaiti restaurant.
   b. Yes, but they're so expensive.
   c. No, not at all. I eat them all the time in Japan.　　　　（　）

4. a. Summer can be quite hot, so I would avoid it then.
   b. He's been doing quite well lately.
   c. I have to come back by seven o'clock tonight.　　　　　（　）

5. a. He trains on a bicycle in the desert.
   b. No, but I would like to see what it's like.
   c. They are much bigger than I thought.　　　　　　　　　（　）

Notes for Reading
　　garment「(長い) 衣服、衣類」　**attire**「服装、装い」　**blazing sun**「焼け付くような日差し」　**strenuous**「骨が折れる、努力を要する」　**rigorously**「きびしく」

Unit 10

RUSSIA:

A New Cultural Stream

【Cultural Recognition】

1 写真を参考にして、次の出だしの英文に続く内容となるよう正しくパラグラフを構成しなさい。

　　Starbucks Coffee opened its first shop in Russia on September 6, 2007. A symbol of capitalism had at last succeeded in invading the former bastion of communism.

A. As early as 1997, Starbucks had already seen that there was plenty of room for coffee shops in Russia, more so than in other European countries, in fact. But they had to wait a few years until the Russian economy began to pick up again.

B. As for the menu, the basic coffee drinks are the same as everywhere else in the world, but the sandwiches and baked items are adapted for local tastes. A Russian Starbucks offers a mushroom-and-cheese sandwich, for example.

C. The company successfully entered Russia at the height of an oil-driven economic boom when average incomes were rising approximately 25 percent annually in dollar terms.

　　　　　　　　　　　　　　1. (　) → 2. (　) → 3. (　)

❷ 前の問題で理解した内容にもとづいて、次の各英文の内容が正しければTを、誤っていればFを選びなさい。

1. T F　A Starbucks coffee shop in Russia might be regarded as a symbol of capitalism.
2. T F　Starbucks forced Russia to close the door on communism.
3. T F　In 2007, the Russian economy was in good condition, with the Russian people enjoying about a 25 percent annual increase in income on average.
4. T F　Starbucks offers its Russian customers a special, local-oriented drinks menu.
5. T F　The food menu, however, is basically the same as that of a shop in Japan, for example.

1. (　) 2. (　) 3. (　) 4. (　) 5. (　)

【Cultural Awareness】　次の英文を読んで下記の各設問に答えなさい。　29

In 1957, the Soviet Union became the first nation to succeed in launching an artificial satellite. This success marked the start of the "Space Race" between the Soviet Union and the United States. The race lasted more than 20 years and became an important part of the cultural, technological, and ideological rivalry between the two nations. But towards the end of the 1970s, the race slowed down, and was gradually replaced by joint missions, with the Soviet space craft *Soyuz* eventually docking in space with America's *Apollo*. By the turn of the 21st century, this collaboration had led to the realization of the International Space Station, which is serviced primarily by the U.S. space shuttle, the Russian manned spacecraft *Soyuz*, and the unmanned spacecraft *Progress*.　(125 words)

❸ 上記の文の内容を最も適切に表していると思われる主題を選びなさい。

1. Russian Dominance in the Space Race
2. The Road to the International Space Station
3. The World's First Artificial Satellite
4. Twenty Years of Rivalry　(　)

4 下線部のアルファベットは、それぞれの英文定義にもとづく語を自由に並べ換えたものです。正しい語を空欄に綴りなさい。

1. chalnu (v)　　→　(　　　　　　　　)
   to send something into the air or into space

2. ecar (n)　　→　(　　　　　　　　)
   a competition between runners, horses, vehicles, etc.

3. llabcoortea (v)　　→　(　　　　　　　　)
   to work together on an activity or project

【**Cultural Interaction**】　次の対話文を読んでから下記の各設問に答えなさい。　CD 30

背景情報 ‖ 日本の高校でＡＬＴとして英語を教えることになった Natasha はつい先日、着任しました。初めてティーム・ティーチングを行った同僚の智子は彼女の英語力に感嘆しきりです。

Tomoko: Your English is really amazing. Isn't your first language Russian?

Natasha: Well, I am Russian after all, but I studied English while I was a student.

Tomoko: I also studied English, but I don't think my level is anything like yours. ₁(sound / speaker / you / like / native / a / just). Why is that?

Natasha: Well, in school we practiced a lot of listening and speaking. Our teachers made us focus on developing good English pronunciation.

Tomoko: That's great. I want to learn to speak English like you.

Natasha: I think your English is just fine. You can use it to communicate, right? ₂(most / that's / important / what's).

5 上の会話文中の 1, 2 の（　　）内の語を意味が通るように正しく並べ換えなさい。

1. _____

2. _____

6 次の和文を英訳しなさい。

ロシア文学に惹かれて、ロシア語を学ぶ人は多い。

___

【Follow-up Exercises】

7 CDの英文を聴いたのち、その最も適切な応答表現の記号を答えなさい。　🎧 31

1. a. There are many gift shops in Moscow.
   b. I like this one the best. You should buy it.
   c. Most people like T-shirts.　　　　　　　　　　　　　　　( )

2. a. I met him last year on a bus in St. Petersburg.
   b. We read about it in my Russian history class.
   c. You should check on the Internet.　　　　　　　　　　　( )

3. a. She works at the information booth at the station.
   b. Okay. I'll call the travel agency later on to get the details.
   c. I think we'll find him in the park.　　　　　　　　　　　( )

4. a. It's for Olga.
   b. We had a nice glass of wine together at the hotel.
   c. Well, we heard how much you like Russian vodka.　　　( )

5. a. This one will take you to the Kremlin.
   b. It's near the Black Sea, I think.
   c. The bus station is across town.　　　　　　　　　　　　( )

___

Notes for Reading

　bastion of communism「共産主義の砦」　**pick up**「回復する、上向く」　**at the height of**「～の絶頂期に」
　an oil-driven economic boom「石油主導の経済景気」　**ideological rivalry**「イデオロギーの対立」
　Soyuz [sóju:z]「ソユーズ（ソ連・ロシアの宇宙船の名前、「連邦」を意味するロシア語）」

Notes for Listening

　St. Petersburg [séint pí:terzbə:g]「サンクトペテルブルグ（ロシア北西部、フィンランド湾の奥に位置する同国第二の都市）」　**Kremlin** [krémlin]「クレムリン宮殿（モスクワにある旧皇居、ロシア政府の官庁として用いられる。旧ソ連政府を意味することもある）」　**Black Sea**「黒海」

Unit 11

SPAIN:
A New Trend in Culture

【Cultural Recognition】

1 写真を参考にして、次の出だしの英文に続く内容となるよう正しくパラグラフを構成しなさい。

　　In Spain, the number of civil wedding ceremonies held at city offices or at commercial wedding halls keeps on rising, but some couples still get married in church. After the ceremony, however, no matter where it is held, the wedding banquet is usually held in a restaurant.

A.　During most of the meal, guests are free to enjoy chatting with other guests.

B.　After the meal, the bride and groom begin to dance to music. The guests follow them onto the dance floor and everyone dances until late at night.

C.　Recently, it has become the custom for young guests to wave their napkins when the newlyweds enter the banquet hall and to keep waving them until the bride and groom are seated at their table.

1. (　) → 2. (　) → 3. (　)

❷ 前の問題で理解した内容にもとづいて、次の各英文の内容が正しければ T を、誤っていれば F を選びなさい。

1. T F　The number of Spanish wedding ceremonies held at churches is increasing.
2. T F　After the wedding ceremony, new couples usually have a wedding banquet in a private home.
3. T F　During the banquet, the guests must usually keep quiet and listen to speeches.
4. T F　After the meal, the newlyweds ask several guests to dance with them.
5. T F　These days, when the newly married couple enter the hall, young guests stand up and applaud them.

1. (　) 2. (　) 3. (　) 4. (　) 5. (　)

【Cultural Awareness】　次の英文を読んで下記の各設問に答えなさい。　CD 32

Bullfighting has long been a sport that combines courage and technique on the part of the bullfighter. This time-honored tradition has usually been associated with masculinity. But recently, some new trends have appeared. For example, several female bullfighters have made their debut, with Christina Sánchez, the first female bullfighter, and Mari Paz Vega among them. Both women are striving to get to a higher position. In addition, there are now many different nationalities among the bullfighters. British, French, and Russian bullfighters, as well as some Japanese, have joined the competition. Right now a Japanese bullfighter is aiming at becoming a "matador," the highest position—the "yokozuna" of bullfighting. (109 words)

❸ 上記の文の内容を最も適切に表していると思われる主題を選びなさい。

1. Female Bullfighters
2. New Trends in Bullfighting
3. The History of Bullfighting
4. Foreign Bullfighters

(　)

47

4
下線部のアルファベットは、それぞれの英文定義にもとづく語を自由に並べ換えたものです。正しい語を空欄に綴りなさい。

1. <u>gourace</u> (n)　→　(　　　　　)
   the quality shown by someone who decides to do something difficult or dangerous

2. <u>scmulintyia</u> (n)　→　(　　　　　)
   the quality or condition of being male

3. <u>onmpeticoti</u> (n)　→　(　　　　　)
   a situation in which two or more people are trying to get the same thing

【Cultural Interaction】
次の対話文を読んでから下記の各設問に答えなさい。　33

背景情報 ║ 友人のフラメンコダンサー Anabelle を訪ねてスペインへやってきた久美子は、すっかりとその華麗な踊りと衣装に魅せられ、Anabelle から手ほどきを受けています。

Kumiko:　Your flamenco dancing is so beautiful. When did you begin practicing?

Anabelle:　When I was a young girl. 1.(my / used / sister / teach / my / me / and / to / aunt).

Kumiko:　I notice that you always wear a traditional flamenco dress, but your sister often wears a two-piece outfit. Are both styles popular?

Anabelle:　Yes, but many younger dancers today like wearing sleeker clothing in order to give better expression to their dance movements.

Kumiko:　Wow, flamenco really is a beautiful art form. Do you think you could show me some of the dance movements sometime?

Anabelle:　Sure. I would be glad to. My sister and I have plenty of dresses for you to try on. Let's see if 2.(one / to / you / for / find / can / we / wear).

5
上の会話文中の 1, 2 の（　　）内の語を意味が通るように正しく並べ換えなさい。

1. _____

2. _____

6 次の和文を英訳しなさい。

スペインでは、男性も女性も共に伝統的なフラメンコギターの演奏にあわせてフラメンコを踊るのが大好きです。

【Follow-up Exercises】

7 CDの英文を聴いたのち、その最も適切な応答表現の記号を答えなさい。 🎧 34

1. a. I've only been to Madrid once.
   b. How about this Saturday?
   c. I love playing the flamenco guitar, too.   (   )

2. a. It's an oil painting, I think.
   b. We've been painting since this morning.
   c. It looks like a Picasso.   (   )

3. a. Real Madrid is my favorite team.
   b. They don't need him anymore.
   c. I am. Would you like to go to?   (   )

4. a. I think it's Pedro.
   b. The office is closed tomorrow.
   c. Yes, I have to finish the project today.   (   )

5. a. I don't think she likes cooking.
   b. I know a good place not too far from here.
   c. We need some fresh garlic.   (   )

<u>*Notes for Reading*</u>

keep on rising「上昇（増加）し続ける」　**banquet hall**「披露宴会場」　**groom**「花婿」　**debut**「初登場、デビュー」　**a two-piece outfit**「上下一揃いの衣装」

<u>*Notes for Listening*</u>

Picasso [pikάːsou]「ピカソ（スペイン生まれのフランスの彫刻家、画家。1881-1973）」　**Real Madrid**「レアル・マドリード（スペインのプロサッカークラブ）」

Unit 12

TANZANIA:
Cultural Conflict

【Cultural Recognition】

1 写真を参考にして、次の出だしの英文に続く内容となるよう正しくパラグラフを構成しなさい。

　　The Maasai people of southern Kenya and northern Tanzania are one of the most well-known African ethnic groups.

A. Their distinctive dress, customs, and way of life have made them a popular attraction among tourists, and they are often featured in magazines and articles about East Africa.

B. Only time will tell what the fate of the Maasai people and their traditions will be; for now, their future is still uncertain.

C. Unfortunately, their traditional way of life has become increasingly difficult to maintain, and many tribal leaders are now struggling to find ways to preserve their traditions while balancing the educational needs of their children growing up in the modern world.

1. (　) → 2. (　) → 3. (　)

2 前の問題で理解した内容にもとづいて、次の各英文の内容が正しければTを、誤っていればFを選びなさい。

1. T F   The Maasai people are a big tourist attraction in East Africa.
2. T F   The Maasai people are eager to modernize and change their way of life.
3. T F   The modern world demands new ways of educating Masaai children.
4. T F   The Maasai people want to preserve their culture while adapting to modern times.
5. T F   It is likely that the Maasai people and their culture will survive for a long time.

1. (   ) 2. (   ) 3. (   ) 4. (   ) 5. (   )

【Cultural Awareness】　次の英文を読んで下記の各設問に答えなさい。

These days the Maasai people's dietary habits are being regarded as a nutritious model for Westerners suffering from such modern diseases as diabetes, heart disease, cancer, and so on. But the opposite could be said to be even truer: that it is the Maasais' lifestyle which is being more profoundly influenced by the spread of Western food to their households. For example, research done by the African Dentists Body suggests that dental problems will increase sharply in African countries, including Tanzania, in the next decade. This is because sugar consumption has risen remarkably recently, and Western foods, which are full of refined sugars, have been replacing the traditional dishes. Dr. Tom Ochola, the chairman of the African Dental Association, warns that consumption of sweets, biscuits, and cakes among young people is very worrying, as more than 70 percent of young people suffer from tooth decay.

(145 words)

3 上記の文の内容を最も適切に表していると思われる主題を選びなさい。

1. How to Prevent Tooth Decay in Africa
2. Popular Sweets in Tanzania
3. Modern Diseases in Western Countries
4. Changes in the Dietary Habits of the Maasai People   (   )

4 下線部のアルファベットは、それぞれの英文定義にもとづく語を自由に並べ換えたものです。正しい語を空欄に綴りなさい。

1. adsbetie (n) → (　　　　　　　　)
   a medical condition in which someone has too much sugar in his/her blood

2. idsetnt (n) → (　　　　　　　　)
   a person who is qualified to examine and treat people's teeth

3. ugras (n) → (　　　　　　　　)
   a sweet substance that is used to sweeten food and drinks

【Cultural Interaction】 次の対話文を読んでから下記の各設問に答えなさい。

背景情報 ‖ 音楽大学に通う大介は、タンザニア大使館で働く友人 Abuu の職場を訪問し、タンザニア打楽器の手作りの伝統について話を聞きました。

Daisuke: Are all these traditional African drums made by hand?

Abuu: Yes, they are. My father and uncle have been making drums like this for many years. They learned the art from my grandfather, and he learned it from his father.

Daisuke: Sounds like your family has been making drums for generations.

Abuu: That's right. It's been our way of life for a long time. Our goal is 1.(keep / culture / our / within / to / tradition / alive / this).

Daisuke: That's good to hear. Do many young people here still enjoy playing traditional music and dancing?

Abuu: Some do. But unfortunately, there are an increasing number of people 2.(important / tradition / who / than / think / modernizing / is / more).

5 上の会話文中の 1, 2 の (　) 内の語を意味が通るように正しく並べ換えなさい。

1. _____

2. _____

6 次の和文を英訳しなさい。

アフリカ音楽は多彩なリズムに特徴があることでよく知られています。

_____

【Follow-up Exercises】

7 CDの英文を聴いたのち、その最も適切な応答表現の記号を答えなさい。　CD 37

1.　a. Yes, we are trying to protect our culture.
　　b. It should leave in about 15 minutes.
　　c. It was just across from the post office.　　　　　　　　　　（　　）

2.　a. His daughter is coming to visit.
　　b. He is hoping to go the day after tomorrow.
　　c. It was really a great decision to come here.　　　　　　　　（　　）

3.　a. Last year, at my university.
　　b. I think next week.
　　c. Just a few months ago.　　　　　　　　　　　　　　　　　（　　）

4.　a. Sorry, but there are no vacancies.
　　b. If possible, non-smoking.
　　c. I don't think there's enough space.　　　　　　　　　　　　（　　）

5.　a. Sorry, I didn't know you were waiting in line.
　　b. I had to buy some coffee on the way.
　　c. It took me over two hours.　　　　　　　　　　　　　　　（　　）

Notes for Reading

　　tribal leader(s)「部族長」　**dietary habit(s)**「食習慣」　**the African Dentists Body**「アフリカ歯科医師団体」
　　tooth decay「虫歯」

Notes for Listening

　　across from「〜の反対側に」　**in line**「一列に並んで」

Unit 13

THAILAND:
The National Symbol

【Cultural Recognition】

① 写真を参考にして、次の出だしの英文に続く内容となるよう正しくパラグラフを構成しなさい。

　　In Thailand, elephants are closely connected to the people. They are revered and cherished as a sacred animal.

A. If you take a close look at Thailand on a world map, you will find that the country is shaped like an elephant's head.

B. During wars in ancient times, the king always rode atop an elephant to lead the army into battle, proving that elephants have long been a symbol of courage and pride.

C. It may be a mere coincidence, but the Thai people are very proud of this geographical wonder.

1. (　) → 2. (　) → 3. (　)

2 前の問題で理解した内容にもとづいて、次の各英文の内容が正しければTを、誤っていればFを選びなさい。

1. T F　To the Thai people, the elephant has religious significance.
2. T F　It is no coincidence that the shape of Thailand on a map is similar to that of an elephant's head.
3. T F　Because elephants are sacred, no one would ever ride one.
4. T F　In the past, Thai kings enjoyed watching battles while sitting on an elephant.
5. T F　The connection between the Thai people and elephants goes back to ancient times.

1. (　) 2. (　) 3. (　) 4. (　) 5. (　)

【Cultural Awareness】　次の英文を読んで下記の各設問に答えなさい。　　38

In Thailand, the garuda is the national emblem and is used as a symbol of the royal family and authority. Have you ever seen a garuda? Well, don't go looking for one in the zoo, because the garuda is a mythical being from Buddhism and Hinduism. The garuda, known as the king of birds, is part man and part bird, with a human body and arms, a demon-like face, and a bird's legs, wings, and tail. You can find many garuda statues and images all around Thailand. Walking through the streets of Bangkok, you'll sometimes see companies with the Royal Garuda Emblem displayed on their buildings. The emblem is awarded to companies as a sign of royal approval, and means that the companies are highly reliable and honorable.　(127 words)

3 上記の文の内容を最も適切に表していると思われる主題を選びなさい。

1. Thailand's Mythical Symbol
2. Thai Business Awards
3. The National Religions of Thailand
4. The Importance of the Royal Family for the Thai People　　(　)

4 下線部のアルファベットは、それぞれの英文定義にもとづく語を自由に並べ換えたものです。正しい語を空欄に綴りなさい。

1. lembme (n) → (   )
   something representing or symbolizing something else

2. etstau (n) → (   )
   a figure made of stone, metal, plastic, or wood

3. lerlaebi (adj) → (   )
   capable of being trusted or depended on

【Cultural Interaction】　次の対話文を読んでから下記の各設問に答えなさい。　39

背景情報 ┃ 観光旅行でタイを訪れている浩は、現地ツアーコンダクターである Niran の案内で、ムエタイ（タイ式ボクシング）の試合観戦に初めて行きました。

Niran: Are you enjoying the Muay Thai matches?

Hiroshi: Yes, I sure am. They are so exciting. 1.(do / how / so / become / strong / to / fighters / the / train)?

Niran: They practice all day every day. Muay Thai is basically their whole life. It's almost a religion in this country. People love the sport and take it very seriously.

Hiroshi: Wow! Have you ever practiced it?

Niran: No, but my cousin does. He trains at a famous gym not far from here. If you want, we can visit his gym tomorrow, and maybe he'll give you a Muay Thai lesson.

Hiroshi: That sounds great. I hope I don't hurt myself, though. 2.(haven't / in / I / exercised / ages).

5 上の会話文中の 1, 2 の（　　）内の語を意味が通るように正しく並べ換えなさい。

1. _____

2. _____

6 次の和文を英訳しなさい。

空港の土産物屋で小さなガルーダの像を買いました。

___

【Follow-up Exercises】

7 CDの英文を聴いたのち、その最も適切な応答表現の記号を答えなさい。 ♪40

1. a. She and I had jasmine rice for lunch.
   b. Yes. It was a bit spicy, but the shrimp was excellent.
   c. Yes, he's great. He's my favorite chef. ( )

2. a. Traditional Thai dancing. Would you like to give it a try?
   b. Yes, he practices very hard every day.
   c. I'm sorry. I'm not used to so much exercise. ( )

3. a. Not in Thailand.
   b. Yes, I had a very bad headache yesterday.
   c. Yes, the shrine is beautiful. ( )

4. a. It's called Muay Thai. It's an exciting sport.
   b. I'm thinking of becoming a monk.
   c. I like watching the fights at the arena with friends. ( )

5. a. I think they serve coconut milk cocktails.
   b. I'm not sure. It may not even be in Bangkok.
   c. I'm going, but I can't stay there very long. ( )

___

<u>Notes for Reading</u>

revere「～を崇拝する」 **atop**「～の背中に」 **authority**「権威」 **mythical being**「想像上の存在」 **approval**「承認」 **honorable**「尊敬に値する、立派な」 **Muay Thai**「タイ式ボクシング、ムエタイ」 **hurt oneself**「けがをする」

<u>Notes for Listening</u>

jasmine rice「ジャスミン米（タイの高級香り米、ジャスミンの花のように白いことからこの名前がついた。特にジャスミンの香りがするわけではない）」 **monk**「僧侶」 **cocktail**「カクテル」

Unit 14

THE UNITED KINGDOM:
Ghosts, Fireworks, and Pubs

【Cultural Recognition】

1 写真を参考にして、次の出だしの英文に続く内容となるよう正しくパラグラフを構成しなさい。

　　While ghosts are generally feared or not talked about in Japan, they have a rather positive image in UK culture.

A. Interestingly, there are so-called ghost tours in various places around the UK which attract not only tourists from outside the country but British people as well.

B. For example, it is said that old houses with ghost stories are more valuable than those without, and that pubs are more popular if they have a haunted past.

C. During the tour, a ghost-tour guide, who is an expert on ghosts and is usually dressed in a top hat and frock coat, guides participants to historical sites while telling them about the ghosts that inhabit them.

1. (　) → 2. (　) → 3. (　)

❷ 前の問題で理解した内容にもとづいて、次の各英文の内容が正しければ T を、誤っていれば F を選びなさい。

1. T F Most people in Japan regard ghosts as something favorable.
2. T F Old buildings with ghost stories behind them tend to be more expensive in the UK.
3. T F Ghost tours in the UK are popular only among foreign tourists.
4. T F Ghost-tour guides have a thorough knowledge of the historical sites.
5. T F Ghost tours take place in various places around the UK.

1. (　)　2. (　)　3. (　)　4. (　)　5. (　)

【Cultural Awareness】 次の英文を読んで下記の各設問に答えなさい。　41

Every year on November 5, you can see and hear fireworks all around the UK. That day is called Guy Fawkes Night, which was established to commemorate the failed Gunpowder Plot against Parliament by a group of Catholics in 1605. The day was named after the most famous plotter, Guy Fawkes. Today, Guy Fawkes Night is a chance for people to have fun. Setting off fireworks is an integral part of the celebration. People also build big bonfires and burn life-sized effigies of Guy Fawkes. On this cold night in November, eating warm food such as jacket potatoes is another attraction. This special day was officially set aside so that the Gunpowder Plot would never be repeated. Isn't it ironic that people now use gunpowder to have a good time on that day?

(133 words)

❸ 上記の文の内容を最も適切に表していると思われる主題を選びなさい。

1. Guy Fawkes Night
2. Bonfires and Effigies
3. History of the Gunpowder Plot
4. The Catholic Uprising

(　)

4 下線部のアルファベットは、それぞれの英文定義にもとづく語を自由に並べ換えたものです。正しい語を空欄に綴りなさい。

1. optltre (n) → (　　　　　　　　)
   a person who secretly plans with others to do something illegal

2. rboenfie (n) → (　　　　　　　　)
   a fire that is made outdoors, usually to burn rubbish

3. tnerilga (adj) → (　　　　　　　　)
   necessary and important

【Cultural Interaction】 次の対話文を読んでから下記の各設問に答えなさい。　42

背景情報 ｜ イギリス留学中の健二は、友人の Simon に連れられて初めてパブを訪れようとしています。単なる居酒屋だと思っていた健二にとって、Simon から耳にする情報は驚きの連続です。

Simon: While you are here in London, how about coming with me to one of the oldest and most famous pubs in all of England?

Kenji: That sounds like a great idea. I have never been to a real English pub. I hear 1.(meet / people / are / they / great / places / to) and socialise.

Simon: That's right. In England, people often go to pubs to relax and mingle with the crowd. It's a great way 2.(end / to / hard / a / day / work / of).

Kenji: Are there also pubs in the countryside?

Simon: Yes. In fact, in some rural areas, the pub is the most important place in town. It is often used as a community centre, church and post office. Actually, the word "pub" is an abbreviation for "public house."

Kenji: I did not know that. That's very interesting. I look forward to going.

5 上の会話文中の 1, 2 の (　　) 内の語を意味が通るように正しく並べ換えなさい。

1. _____

2. _____

6 次の和文を英訳しなさい。

旅行中、私たちは伝統的な英国パブに立ち寄って昼食をとるつもりです。

___

【Follow-up Exercises】

7 CDの英文を聴いたのち、その最も適切な応答表現の記号を答えなさい。 43

1. a. No, I'm not.
   b. That would be lovely.
   c. They don't like it. ( )

2. a. Yes, just in case.
   b. I'm afraid not.
   c. No, you should take one. ( )

3. a. Ten kilometres from here.
   b. It leaves in 30 minutes.
   c. Two pounds for a single ticket. ( )

4. a. That's absurd.
   b. The queue starts over there.
   c. Ages, it looks like. ( )

5. a. The spicier the better.
   b. A pint of bitter, please.
   c. Just some crisps, please. ( )

___

Notes for Reading

set(ting) off fireworks「花火を打ち上げる」　bonfire(s)「(宗教的祭事などのためにたく) 大きなかがり火」　socialise「〜と交流する」　mingle with the crowd「多くの人々と談笑する」

Notes for Listening

absurd「とんでもない」　queue [kjúː]「(順番を待つ人々の) 列」　pint「英国で用いられている液量の単位、約0.57リットル」　bitter「ビター (英国ビールの種類、苦みが強い)」　crisp(s)「ポテトチップス (通例複数形で使用する)」

Unit 15

THE UNITED STATES:
Security Measures

【Cultural Recognition】

1 写真を参考にして、次の出だしの英文に続く内容となるよう正しくパラグラフを構成しなさい。

　　Considering the current situation in America, with the number of crimes increasing each year, it is no wonder that people are looking for a safer housing environment.

A. However, the gates and walls also send out the message, "We don't want any outsiders entering here."

B. Thus, it is quite understandable that more and more American families are choosing to live in a "gated community" that offers them a greater sense of security.

C. This is a residential community that has controlled entrances for pedestrians, bicycles, and automobiles, and that is usually enclosed inside walls and fences.

1. ( )　→　2. ( )　→　3. ( )

❷ 前の問題で理解した内容にもとづいて、次の各英文の内容が正しければTを、誤っていればFを選びなさい。

1. T F   America is growing safer year by year.
2. T F   A "gated community" is a housing complex surrounded by gates and walls.
3. T F   People choose gated communities because they like the feeling of being cut off from society.
4. T F   Only those people, cars, and bicycles that have permission are allowed to enter a gated community.
5. T F   Some people might be offended by the elitist message these communities send out.

1. (   )   2. (   )   3. (   )   4. (   )   5. (   )

【Cultural Awareness】　次の英文を読んで下記の各設問に答えなさい。　　44

In the U.S., security systems have been installed in many buildings in order to prevent crime. The most renowned system uses infrared rays to detect slight temperature changes when someone tries to enter a building. The system sends an alarm to the nearest police station, and a police car or police helicopter soon arrives at the site. If someone triggers the system by mistake, he or she has to enter a password or code using a key pad mounted on the wall of the building to shut the alarm off. Nowadays, however, the systems are so delicate that they sometimes go off even when barely touched. According to an old proverb, "A wise man never courts danger." At any rate, if you're going to live in the U.S., you'd better have a certain knowledge of security systems.

(137 words)

❸ 上記の文の内容を最も適切に表していると思われる主題を選びなさい。

1. How Infrared Rays Work
2. Crime and Punishment in the United States
3. Security Systems in the United States
4. Wall-mounted Sensors   (   )

63

4 下線部のアルファベットは、それぞれの英文定義にもとづく語を自由に並べ換えたものです。正しい語を空欄に綴りなさい。

1. tectde (v) → (　　　　　）
   to use equipment to find something or discover that something is present

2. larma (n) → (　　　　　）
   an automatic device that warns you of danger

3. asdspwro (n) → (　　　　　）
   a secret word or phrase that you must know in order to enter a place

【Cultural Interaction】 次の対話文を読んでから下記の各設問に答えなさい。

背景情報 ║ 米国に留学中の浩二は、ホームステイ先の Eric とすっかり意気投合し、今や何でも話し合える仲になっています。

Koji: I hear your brother works at a high school. What does he do there?

Eric: 1.(guard / as / on / security / a / works / campus / he) and patrols the student parking lot.

Koji: Student parking lot? Are students allowed to drive to school?

Eric: Yes, many of the juniors and seniors come to school by car. My brother has to make sure that 2.(assigned / parking / park / their / they / space / in) and that they obey the rules. If they don't, he gives them a parking violation ticket.

Koji: I can't imagine high-school students driving to school. It would never happen back home in Japan. Is it quite common here?

Eric: Yes. Since the driving age is sixteen and many students have to rush to part-time jobs after school, more than half of them drive.

5 上の会話文中の 1, 2 の (　　) 内の語を意味が通るように正しく並べ換えなさい。

1. _____

2. _____

❻ 次の和文を英訳しなさい。

外国で車を運転しようと考えるならば、事前に国際運転免許書を手に入れておくべきです。

【Follow-up Exercises】

❼ CDの英文を聴いたのち、その最も適切な応答表現の記号を答えなさい。　🎧 46

1. a. The Statue of Liberty was built in 1886.
   b. Beats me. I'm not from around here.
   c. It's a battery for my computer.　　　　　　　　　　　　（　）

2. a. She came last night after eight.
   b. I had to visit a friend in the hospital.
   c. You can wear Levis if you want. It's very casual.　　　（　）

3. a. I don't know. You know her better than I do.
   b. Thank you, but I am the vice president.
   c. The day after tomorrow.　　　　　　　　　　　　　　　（　）

4. a. We have to stop at the gate and ask for permission.
   b. I've lived here for three years.
   c. The exit's over there.　　　　　　　　　　　　　　　　（　）

5. a. We played baseball all day.
   b. The meeting should be finished soon.
   c. If not, I'll get a doggy bag.　　　　　　　　　　　　　（　）

<u>Notes for Reading</u>

a greater sense of security「より大きな安心感」　**pedestrian(s)**「歩行者」　**infrared ray(s)**「赤外線」
trigger「～を作動させる」　**barely**「わずかに」

<u>Notes for Listening</u>

beats me「それには参った、わかりません」　**Levis**「リーバイス；ジーンズの商標」　**doggy bag**「（レストランでの食べ残しを客が持ち帰るための）持ち帰り袋」